EVERY
Thanksgiving
DAY

living a life full of gratitude

A Soul Inspired Bible Study and Journal

SWEET TO THE SOUL
ministries

CONTENTS

PLANTING THE
SEEDS OF GOD'S WORD
IN OUR HEART AND
WATERING THEM WITH PRAYER
GROWS THE MOST BEAUTIFUL
blooms of thanksgiving.

Jana Kennedy-Spicer

Introduction

Just a few weeks ago, my husband and I were enjoying some time away in the mountains of New Mexico. The bright golden color of aspen trees with changing leaves combined with the cool crisp air was soul refreshing for this Texas girl.

Although it was still hot at home, there in the mountains, my favorite season was in full display.

Autumn. Ahhhh.

Yes, my favorite season. But not for the weather, although the cooler temps are very welcome after 100° summer days. And not for the colors, even though there is nothing like the beauty of the fiery red and golden leaves fluttering in the breeze.

No autumn is my favorite time of year because as the season changes, it seems attitudes also change and a sense of "gathering" sets in as the holidays are just around the corner.

Thanksgiving and Christmas.

True thanksgiving, though, is so much more than a holiday or a by-product of changing seasons.

True thanksgiving is a heart condition displayed in our normal day to day life.

*True thanksgiving is **everyday** thanksgiving.*

When we say "thank you" to someone is it typically for something - something they've said that made us feel good or something they've done which we appreciate. This is a lovely and right expression. But this isn't the type of thanksgiving we are called to by God's Word.

Biblical thanksgiving is much deeper than a mere expression or note card.

"Give thanks in all circumstances,
for this is the will of God in Christ Jesus for you."
1 Thessalonians 5:18
Biblical thanksgiving is not based on our circumstances, it is *in spite of our circumstances.*

"Giving thanks always and for everything to God the Father
in the name of our Lord Jesus Christ."
Ephesians 5:20
Biblical thanksgiving is not an occasional feeling or spoken word, it is *an always attitude.*

These scriptures teach us that:
1. True thanksgiving is present in all of our circumstances— good or bad, easy or hard, beneficial or costly.
2. True thanksgiving is present in all of our days— short or long, calm or stressful. Celebratory or mournful.
3. True thanksgiving is *everyday thanksgiving.*

Soul Friends, I would love for you to join me on this 31-day journey through the Bible as we dive soul deep each day in to God's Word to learn how we can live a life of *everyday thanksgiving.*

Everyday Thanksgiving — Living a Life Full of Gratitude

Scripture Reading List

1. 1 Thessalonians 2:13
2. Colossians 3:17
3. Philippians 1:3
4. Psalm 79:13
5. 1 Chronicles 16:35
6. 1 Timothy 2:1
7. Isaiah 51:3
8. Psalm 118:21
9. Romans 1:8
10. 1 Thessalonians 3:9
11. Daniel 2:23
12. Philippians 4:6
13. Psalm 95:2
14. 1 Chronicles 16:34
15. 1 Timothy 1:12
16. Ephesians 5:4
17. Psalm 109:30
18. Revelation 11:17
19. 1 Corinthians 15:57
20. Colossians 3:15
21. Luke 2:38
22. Psalm 75:1
23. 1 Chronicles 23:30
24. 2 Corinthians 9:11-12
25. Jeremiah 30:19
26. Psalm 142:7
27. Romans 6:17
28. 1 Chronicles 29:13
29. 2 Thessalonians 1:3
30. Luke 17:15-16
31. Psalm 28:7

AND NOW WE
thank you
our God AND
Praise YOUR
Glorious
NAME

FIRST
CHRONICLES
29:13

JLK

How to Use This Study

In this study booklet, you have three sections.

In **SECTION ONE** you have a page for 7 of the scriptures on our reading list. Go at your own pace, whether a scripture a day or a week, or even several a day.

• On each scripture's page you'll see 5 sections.

READ : Read the scripture. Read it in context including the scriptures before and after, maybe even the whole chapter. Look it up in multiple translations. Then, write out the scripture in your own words, personalizing it specific to you and your current situation.

REFLECT : Use your Bible study sources (commentaries, dictionaries, etc or BibleHub.com) to learn more about the scripture. Make notations about what stood out to you.

RELATE : How does this scripture relate to you personally or your life situation? What does God want you to know from this scripture? How does it speak God's reassurances to you? Make all of these notations in this section.

REMEMBER : What is the one or main thing about the scripture which you want to remember?

PRAY : Conclude your study time by writing a prayer to God. Maybe incorporate portions of the scripture. Praise God and thank Him for the blessings in your life.

If you're like me, you may need more writing room, so keep some blank paper handy. Use the blank pages included to study additional scriptures.

In **SECTION TWO** you will find three devotionals from myself and my friend Jodie Barrett about how we can we can learn to live a life full of thanksgiving.

My prayer is that the devotions and challenges — *Thankful for You, Entering His Gates and Recounting Your Wonderous Deeds* — will inspire, challenge and encourage all of us to seek a humble position before God which enables us to change our perspective to recognize all that we have with a heart of gratitude.

In **SECTION THREE** you will find the full year *Everyday Thanksgiving Challenge Journal.* Use these pages throughout the year to document your gratitude every day. Take time to daily pause and intentionally express gratitude for what God has done that day.

Included are several additional scriptures for study and reflections as well as some specific encouragements and challenges to help us win the war of our words.

On the **Prayer Journal** pages, select one or two of the scriptures from each session to personalize and pray back to God.

Also you'll find lots of space to journal or get creative and let your soul be inspired.

read   "And whatever you do, in word or deed, do everything in the name of the Lord Jesus, giving
thanks to God the Father through him."

Colossians 3:17

reflect

Everyday Thanksgiving — Living a Life Full of Gratitude

relate

remember

pray

read   "But we your people, the sheep of your pasture, will give thanks to you forever; from generation to generation we will recount your praise."

Psalm 79:13

reflect

Everyday Thanksgiving — Living a Life Full of Gratitude

relate

remember

pray

read   "Oh give thanks to the LORD, for he is good; for his steadfast love endures forever! "

1 Chronicles 16:34

reflect

relate

remember

pray

read   "With my mouth I will give great thanks to the
LORD; I will praise him in the midst of the
throng."

Psalm 109:30

reflect

Everyday Thanksgiving — Living a Life Full of Gratitude

relate

remember

pray

read   "But thanks be to God, who gives us the victory through our Lord Jesus Christ."

1 Corinthians 15:57

reflect

Everyday Thanksgiving — Living a Life Full of Gratitude

relate

remember

pray

read "Out of them shall come songs of thanksgiving, and the voices of those who celebrate. I will multiply them, and they shall not be few; I will make them honored, and they shall not be small."

Jeremiah 30:19

reflect

relate

remember

pray

read   "The LORD is my strength and my shield; in him my heart trusts, and I am helped; my heart exults, and with my song I give thanks to him."

Psalm 28:7

reflect

Everyday Thanksgiving — Living a Life Full of Gratitude

relate

remember

pray

read

reflect

relate

remember

pray

read

reflect

relate

remember

pray

What Inspired Your Soul This Week?

What Inspired Your Soul This Week?

Prayer Journal

GIVE thanks WITH A grateful Heart

1 THESSALONIANS 5:18

Thankful for You

"I thank my God in all my remembrance of you."
Philippians 1:3

When I read today's scripture, it immediately brought to my heart sweet memories of my dad and my brother. They have both passed on to heaven so all I have of them today are my memories of life with them.

You may have experienced something similar, remembering someone no longer in your life.

Our verse today is found in the opening of the Apostle Paul's letter to the church at Philippi. This church held a special place in Paul's heart because it was the first church he founded in Europe.

The meaning in Paul's words is clear: when he thinks of the church and its members, he is thankful to God. And he says further in the next verse that praying for them brings him joy.

*"always in every prayer of mine for you
making my prayer with joy,"*
Philippians 1:4

Some scriptures we need to dive deep to extract God's rich meaning, but today it is right there floating on top. Now, that doesn't mean it's light weight or shallow. Oh, no. It's like a beautiful water lily – in full bloom on the surface of calm waters but anchored down deep in the rich soil below the water.

And that's how I want this Word of God to be in my life – planted soul deep and creating beautiful blooms in my everyday life.

I Thank My God

For us to thank God, for anything, we must first realize that all things – EVERY thing – we have is from God.

"The earth is the LORD's and the fullness thereof,
the world and those who dwell therein,"
Psalm 24:1

We can be so selfish, living our lives in a manner where we see everything and everyone revolving around us. Everything is here for me and everything is mine. That sounds harsh, but we are selfish at heart because of our sin nature. It's not something we're taught; we are born with this nature. No? Try taking that toy or blanket or bottle away from a baby! Ha!

As adults, the best weapon we have in our arsenal to fight this vanity is God's Word. And it tells us that in contrast to our "mine" mentality, everything is not ours. Everything, in fact, is God's

"Every good gift and every perfect gift is from above,
coming down from the Father of lights, with whom there is no
variation or shadow due to change."
James 1:17

If we are blessed to have things and people in our lives, these have been given to us by Him also. That job or promotion that we work hard to achieve, it is a gift from God. That house or car or meal or brand name something or other that we just purchased with "my" money, yes, those also are gifts from God.

So, I must ask myself...

- If everything I have is indeed not mine but God's, why do I not thank Him?

- And if everything I have is not something I have earned or deserve, but is a gift from God, why do I not thank Him?

This is soul deep, friends. This is where the seeds are planted. This is fundamental.

If we truly desire for God to treat the epidemic of ingratitude and entitlement, we must allow Him to do this heart surgery in us. I must allow Him to cut straight to the heart of the problem – in my own heart – and plant the seeds of His Word deep – soul deep.

- Have you found yourself in a cycle of ingratitude?

- What do you think contributes to this heart condition?

- Have you seen the quote, "If all you had tomorrow was what you thanked God for today, what would you have?" - how would you answer?

- Write a prayer to God, tell him how you want your life to be impacted during this study.

In Remembrance of You

Memories. (que the soundtrack)

The older I get, the more I value my memory. Probably because I have a little less each day. I have so many wonderful memories that I love to recall and would go back and visit some of those times or people if I could. But then there's another room in my memory warehouse that I don't like to visit. As beautiful as some memories are, others can be equally not.

In Paul's context, though, he is wanting to encourage the recipients of his letter. He is telling them that he not only remembers them, but that every time he does, he thanks God for them.

How would you feel if that was the opening line of a letter you received? Ok, maybe an email, but all the same, to have someone stop whatever they are doing and take time to tell you that not only are they thinking about you but they are thankful for you. Add the bonus of them thanking God for you because they recognize that you and your relationship are a gift from God?

Make. my. day.

So, I (we) must ask myself...
• When was the last time I made someone's day in this manner?

Let's go back farther.
• When was the last time I thanked God for the people in my life?

And not just the ones who I am happy with or who have done something for me lately.

- When was the last time I thanked God for the difficult, disagreeable sandpaper people in my life?

It seems the road to Everyday Thanksgiving is not a smooth one.

FOR MY LIFE TO CHANGE, *my heart condition must change.*

When I started writing these devotionals, I (boldly?) told God that I didn't want to just make another cute little list focusing on the obvious wonderful things in my life, I wanted this time with Him to go deeper – and friends, He is taking me there.

So, here's my challenge for today – **LIVE IT.**

What value is a "Thank You" if it's never spoken?

CHALLENGE 1

Take time with God to recognize all the people in your life and thank Him specifically for each one. (yes, all and every. Flex those gratitude muscles. If it takes longer than just today, that's ok)

Personalize the following scripture for them, thanking God and adding something specific about this person for which you are thankful.

"Every time I think of you, I give thanks to my God."
Philippians 1:3 NLT

(Example)

Lord, every time I think of _____, I give you thanks for him/her/them because _____

_____

_____.

Amen.

These prayers will make beautiful entries into your journaling and also serve as a reminder of your many blessings.

- Who are you thankful for?
   1.

   2.

   3.

   4.

   5.

   6.

Lord, every time I think of _____, I give

you thanks for him/her/them because _____

_____

_____.

Amen.

Lord, every time I think of _____, I give

you thanks for him/her/them because _____

_____

_____.

Amen.

Lord, every time I think of _____, I give

you thanks for him/her/them because _____

_____

_____.

Amen.

Lord, every time I think of _____, I give

you thanks for him/her/them because _____

_____

_____.

Amen.

CHALLENGE 2

Take a break. Stop. Sit. Write a note to someone – to many someones – and tell them you are thankful for them. Tell them why. And tell them,

> *"Every time I think of you, I give thanks to my God."*
> Philippians 1:3 NLT

Use those journal entries and prayers from the first challenge to create thank you notes. Snail mail has almost been replaced with text messages and emails, but don't we get excited over personal notes in our mail box!

The following pages have some card designs which you can copy, color, add your special note and drop in the mail to brighten someone's day.

As a bonus to this challenge, think of other creative ways to express your gratitude to friends, family, co-workers and others. Let's start an epidemic of thankfulness!

* Leave a note on a co-worker's desk
* Tape an "I'm thankful for you" note on a mirror for your spouse
* Send a favorite treat and special "thank you" to your child's teacher
* Send a card to a personal influencer and thank them for their impact on your life.

• Who else are you thankful for?

• How can you let them know?

Prayer Journal

What Inspired Your Soul This Week?

Entering His Gates

"Enter into his gates with thanksgiving, and into his courts with praise; be thankful to him and bless his name."
Psalm 100:4

Sleeping past the alarm on Sunday morning put us in a rush and between moving at a quicker pace and the morning routine getting out of order, I have to say honestly, we were a little on edge with each other by the time we left the house.

Finally at church, I needed to go one way and he needed to go another, both of us walking away from each other briskly and agitated. By the time I made it to my seat in the worship center, the praise and worship team was already into their second number. As I sat down next to my daughter – her giving me 'the look' – I let out a heavy sigh and joined in on the singing, but my heart was struggling to worship.

In David's Psalm of Praise, when he mentions "His gates" and "His courts" he is referring to the Lord's Temple. But today, we can also apply these words to when we are entering into our churches or worship centers.

When I rushed into "His gates" – our church – that morning, where was my thankfulness?

When I finally made it into "His courts" – our worship center – where was my praise?

Oh, and where were my glasses? Great, now I couldn't even read my Bible.

Needless to say, my communion with God that Sunday was less than stellar. I allowed myself to be distracted by the circumstances of my morning and gave no reverence to the fact that I was entering into God's holy house.

I was focused on me, not Him.

Focusing on Him... isn't that what 'going to church' is all about? It's about Him, God. Not me or my duties, not catching up with friends, not seeing who is/isn't there and what they are wearing. It's not even about what songs we're singing or what passage of scripture is being preached. It's all about Him, *worshiping and praising Him.*

David is reminding us of that in this scripture.

⇒ **"enter His gates with thanksgiving":** for our hearts to be in a position of thanksgiving, we must choose to recognize the blessings provided by God in every situation.

⇒ **"enter His courts with praise":** to truly praise God we must acknowledge in our hearts His position of holiness and His role of savior, provider, redeemer, comforter.

Thanksgiving & Praise
COMPEL US TO FOCUS ON GOD, NOT OURSELVES.

Please don't misunderstand, my worship that morning wasn't hindered because I was running late, it was hindered because I was not really worshipping God at all. My physical body finally got to the church, but my heart and spirit were distracted and not focusing on God at all.

So how can we prepare ourselves for worship?

1. **Have the Proper Perspective:** *We are entering into the presence of the most Holy God.*

   We can become so familiar with our surroundings and routines, that we give no reverence to whom we are meeting with, **God**.

   Nancy DeMoss Wolgemuth says: *"That the holy, powerful, majestic God who fills heaven and earth with His presence and His glory should invite us—tiny, puny, fallen sinners— to come into His presence. That's amazing! It's astonishing!"* *[Enter His Gates with Thanksgiving series]*

   Let's remember that "church" is not about the building, the programs, the pastor, the teachers or socializing with our friends, but rather to worship our Holy God.

- Do you find yourself distracted during worship service?

- What can you do differently to overcome this challenge?

2. **Prepare Our Hearts:** *Spend time in worship and in God's Word.*

Almost every other area of our life we spend time in preparation—before we go to class, before we attend a business meeting, before we take a test, before we make a significant purchase. We prepare for these things because they are important.

- If you know your pastor will be preaching on a particular passage, read these scriptures prior to service.
- Listen to worship music while getting ready and on your way to your church service.
- Spend a few moments in quiet reflective prayer to calm your mind and center your soul with God.

Let's remember to be conscience of how our time prior to the church service can impact our worship during the service, and shift our heart's attention to God before we ever arrive.

- What is your biggest challenge in preparing your heart for worship?

- What can you do differently to overcome this challenge?

3. **Focus on a Single Priority:** *Lay aside all else so we can sit at the feet of God.*

    We all have many responsibilities, including God given assignments, but when God is in our presence, he wants us to focus only on him.

    Remember sisters Mary and Martha? Jesus was in their home, but the sisters reacted differently to his presence. Martha was busy attending to the needs of her guests—a good thing to do in most circumstances. But Mary, chose to set aside her normal household responsibilities to sit at Jesus's feet. What was Jesus' response when Martha complained?

    "Martha, you are anxious and trouble about many things, but only one thing is necessary. Mary has chosen the good portion which will not be taken away from her." Luke 10:41-42

    Let's remember that all of those tasks and responsibilities will wait. In the presence of God, let's be "all in" the presence of God. The tasks and to-dos will still be there after our worship time.

- What is your biggest challenge to focusing during a service?

- What can you do differently to overcome this challenge?

Charles Spurgeon wrote:

*"In all our public service the rendering of thanks must abound;
it is like the incense of the temple, which filled the whole house
with smoke. What better subject for our thoughts in God's
own house than the Lord of the house.
And into his courts with praise. Into whatever court
of the Lord you may enter, let your admission be the subject
of praise: thanks be to God, the innermost court is
now open to believers."*

Friends, God is in His house and wanting eagerly to meet with us! To fellowship with us! When we enter His gates, it's all about Him, not us. So whenever and wherever we go to meet with Him, let's be thankful, let's praise Him, let's bless His holy name; let's leave everything thing else outside and sit at His feet and give Him our full undivided attention, after all, He is giving us His.

Prayer Journal

What Inspired Your Soul This Week?

THESE ARE A FEW OF MY
favorite things....

List some of the reasons
you Praise God's Name:

we thank you our GOD and praise your GLORIOUS name

1 CHRONICLES 29:13

Recounting Your Wondrous Deeds

By Jodie Barrett

"We give thanks to you, O God; we give thanks, for your name is near.
We recount your wondrous deeds."
Psalm 75:1

Grasping hands, we stand in a circle and she says, "Share one thing you are thankful for" and silence fills the room.

It's Thanksgiving Day and we have all gathered to feast, hunt, fellowship, read the sales papers, watch the parade, and yes, give thanks. But every year it's a little awkward when my husband's mom asks the group to share what they are grateful for as we join hands to ask a blessing over the mounds of food.

Why?

It seems simple enough. There is a mound of food in the kitchen and the hands that worked hard preparing; there is the gathering of loved ones, generation to generation.

Thanksgiving should slip from our lips.

So why is it difficult?

Mainly, I think the group just doesn't like to be put on the spot. Talking in a group is not everyone's cup of tea. But if I am honest, I also believe that it's uncomfortable because we don't take time to count our blessings every day. We have become a society that shares our complaint but not our gratitude. Don't worry, I'm speaking about myself as much as anyone and my toes are feeling pinched. I'm the first to admit that when my mouth opens and I hear complaints slip forth I cringe. I catch myself whining and remind myself that praise should be the resounding noise that I share, not complaint.

As Thanksgiving approaches I have a prayer on my heart, *"Lord, help me to be grateful. And Lord let it go beyond one day."*

I Thessalonians 5:18 reads,
"Give thanks in all circumstances; for this is the will of God in Christ Jesus for you."

Several years ago while teaching a women's bible study I giggled at the word "**all**" and so did the rest of the girls. That is a big order, right? Let's consider the things I did during my years as a nurse. I stood in a patient's room while he lost his breakfast right on me as I assisted him out of bed. It's one thing to catch that sort of yuck from your children but another all together from a stranger. Unpleasant, I know, but I really wanted to drive home the point that "all circumstances" brings with it a tall order. All is an enormous word that encompasses a great deal of things that I'm not certain we think to be grateful for each day, yet, God says it's His will for us.

Insert our prayer.
"Lord, help me to be grateful. And Lord let it go beyond one day."

Then consider today's scripture, **"We give thanks to you, O God; we give thanks, for your name is near. We recount your wondrous deeds."**
* ***We***: Those who believe and call your Lord.
* ***Give thanks...for your name is near:*** God is near us always and that is simply enough to be thankful.
* ***Recount your wondrous deeds:*** Start at the beginning and recount the wonderful deeds that God has done.

Striving to obtain a grateful heart that counts blessings 365 days a year takes an intentional shift of our mindset. Count and recount. We must prepare our hearts in advance to focus on the blessings.

An intentional focus of gratitude HELPS DESTROY AN UGLY ATTITUDE OF COMPLAINT.

For instance, go back to my day with my patient. I'm grateful that I held him up while his world was spinning in circles. He was a back surgery patient and a fall to the floor would have been detrimental to his recovery. I'm thankful he and I had time to laugh after I changed clothes. I have counted and continue to recount this time as a blessing.

Just recently our family lost two loved ones in a matter of a week to cancer. It was a tragic set of circumstances. Two funerals, back to back; the grief was heavy. However, as tears flowed, a group of cousins that had drifted apart, gathered to embrace and remember. With that came laughter, hugs, and determination to stay in touch during good times. **Gratitude grew are we spent time together counting past blessings.** Certainly we could have complained, instead we focused our hearts on God being near, even during grief.

This year when my family joins hands and shares a time of awkward silence I hope to burst forth with joy and simply say today's verse, "We give thanks to you, O God; we give thanks, for your name is near. We recount your wondrous deeds."

And then I'll whisper our prayer, *"Lord, help me to be grateful. And Lord let it go beyond one day."*

- How would you answer the question if asked in a room full of others — share one thing you are grateful for?

- Recall a incident which at the time was very difficult or unpleasant.

- Were you thankful at the time?

- Looking back now (like Jodie did) can you find something about the situation to be grateful?

- How can recognizing gratitude in the reflection of this circumstance help you to express thankfulness in current situations?

- Consider a recent or current situation, can you now find an aspect to reflect gratitude for this situation?

Lord,
We come with thanksgiving and a simple prayer for our hearts. Help us be grateful beyond one day. May we be intentional to shift our focus and let praise slip freely from our lips in all circumstances. Forgive us when we get stuck in an ugly attitude of complaint. We know that is not your will for us. When we face the difficult parts of our day help us remember to give thanks while we recount your wondrous deeds. In Christ's name, Amen

What Inspired Your Soul This Week?

Prayer Journal

do not be
ANXIOUS
ABOUT anything BUT IN
EVERYthing
by PRAYER & SUPPLICATION with

Thanksgiving

let your REQUESTS
be made known to God
~ Philippians 4:6 ~

Collecting "SONshine" in a Jar

Do you ever keep score? You know, within your relationships. Sadly, there have been times that I have. Maybe I didn't do it on purpose, but it seems that whenever I am in a conflict with someone, re-counting any little hurtful thing they have said or done just pops up like an unwelcome weed!

And just like weeds in our garden can choke beautiful flowers, these emotional weeds can choke a good relationship.

But what if we changed our scorekeeping and instead of keeping a tally of hurtful things, we began to count and collect thoughtful and kind and loving things. Or like our friend Jodie says: "SONshine".

Jodie writes,
"While walking through a difficult season in our marriage, I began counting SONshine moments each day. INTENTIONALLY looking for the small blessings during a hard time. In my prayer journal I would end my page by drawing a sun and listing my SONshine blessing that I was thankful for. One day it was hearing my husband snore— it was a really hard day but we were still together!"

I love this idea! And I am taking on this challenge! Will y'all join us?

SONSHINE *in a Jar Project*

1. Find a large jar - one that will hold lots of SONshine!
2. Decorate as desired.
3. Keep a pen and pieces of paper, or post it pad, next to your jar for easy access.
4. Place the jar in a prominent location, you will see each day.
5. Everyday, intentionally look for the blessings in your day.
6. Write your SONshine on a piece of paper, fold it up and place it in the jar.
7. Select a date - or multiple dates - for your family to get together and read the SONshine notes with each other.

Psalms of Thanksgiving

In researching the Bible for scriptures to use in our *Everyday Thanksgiving* series, it was difficult to narrow the list from hundreds to only thirty-one. There are so many lessons of being thankful during any circumstances we may face.

If you are like me, then we both love having scripture present during our everyday life. These can be quick reminders and instant access to God's Word to fight the negativity whispered in our ears by the enemy.

So copy or cut out the following page of 7 Psalms of Thanksgiving, and tuck into your Bible or journal or anywhere to keep them handy. And there's plenty of space on the back side of the page to add your own special scriptures.

You can also use this list to commit these scriptures to memory, to arm your heart for the battles from our enemy.

*"Sing praises to the Lord, O you his saints,
and give thanks to his holy name."*
Psalm 30:4

*"We give thanks to you, O God; we give thanks,
for your name is near.
We recount your wondrous deeds."*
Psalm 75:1

*"But we your people, the sheep of your pasture,
will give thanks to you forever; from generation to
generation we will recount your praise."*
Psalm 79:13

*"Let them thank the Lord for his steadfast love,
for his wondrous works to the children of man!"*
Psalm 107:8

*"I thank you that you have answered me and
have become my salvation."*
Psalm 118:21

*"Surely the righteous shall give thanks to your name;
the upright shall dwell in your presence."*
Psalm 140:13

*"Bring me out of prison, that I may give
thanks to your name! The righteous will surround
me, for you will deal bountifully with me."*
Psalm 142:7

More Thanksgiving Scriptures

We your people the sheep of Your pasture .WILL. GIVE THANKS to you FOREVER FROM Generation To GENERATION we WILL recount YOUR praise

PSALM 79:13

Prayer Journal

What Inspired Your Soul This Week?

Challenge Journal

Autumn, my favorite season. October means pumpkin spice every-thing and November means all topics thanksgiving and gratitude.

But what happens in January? And then February? March? April? .....
Do we carry our 'attitude of gratitude' so prominently displayed in November throughout every other month during the year?

This journal looks common, but it's not just a place to make a list of things your are thankful for during November. This *"Everyday Thanksgiving Challenge Journal"* is different because I am throwing out a challenge to you (and me).

CHALLENGE #1: Use this journal for 365 days. Habits may be formed in 30 days or less, but changes of heart are reflected every day after. Everyday thanksgiving stretches well beyond the boundary of a calendar month, it is a heart condition which we live out each and every day. So use this journal for November, and then again for December, and again for January, and so on, and so on.

> *"Give thanks in all circumstances,*
> *for this is the will of God in Christ Jesus for you."*
> 1 Thessalonians 5:18

CHALLENGE #2: Be thankful in all circumstances. True thanks-giving is not dependent on our circumstances. True thanksgiving ex-ists in spite of our circumstance. So the second challenge is to not look for the easy things to be thankful for like friends and family and happy moments. Oh be thankful for those things, but look for the difficult moments and find something thankful in that circumstance. Look toward that difficult person in your life, and find something thankful about that relationship.

*"Giving thanks always and for everything to God the Father
in the name of our Lord Jesus Christ."*
Ephesians 5:20

CHALLENGE #3: Be thankful for everything, everyday. True thanksgiving understands that every happening, every gift, every challenge is from God. So the third challenge is to daily pause and intentionally express gratitude for what God has done that day. Good or bad, happy or sad. It's easy to be thankful when something goes our way or something happens to make us happy, but sometimes God's gift to us is much bigger. We need to always be aware of God in our life and acknowledge that everything we have is from God. It's important for us to recognize these God moments and to give God the glory.

So, are you up for the challenge? You don't have to do this alone. Invite a friend to join you and also accept the challenge. Join our community on-line and let's accept this challenge together! I'll share my Everyday Thanksgiving moments, and you can share some of yours.

Let's encourage others to develop the beautiful heart condition of *Everyday Thanksgiving.*

November

Today I Am Thankful For:

1.

2.

3.

4.

5.

6.

7.

8.

Everyday Thanksgiving — Living a Life Full of Gratitude

9.

10.

11.

12.

13.

14.

15.

16.

17.

18.

19.

20.

21.

22.

23.

24.

25.

26.

Everyday Thanksgiving — Living a Life Full of Gratitude

27.

28.

29.

30.

This month God showed me:

December

Today I Am Thankful For:

1.

2.

3.

4.

5.

6.

7.

8.

9.

10.

11.

12.

13.

14.

15.

16.

17.

18.

19.

20.

21.

22.

23.

24.

25.

26.

27.

28.

29.

30.

31.

This month God showed me:

January

Today I Am Thankful For:

1.

2.

3.

4.

5.

6.

7.

8.

Everyday Thanksgiving — Living a Life Full of Gratitude

9.

10.

11.

12.

13.

14.

15.

16.

17.

18.

19.

20.

21.

22.

23.

24.

25.

26.

27.

28.

29.

30.

31.

This month God showed me:

February

Today I Am Thankful For:

1.

2.

3.

4.

5.

6.

7.

8.

9.

10.

11.

12.

13.

14.

15.

16.

17.

18.

19.

20.

21.

22.

23.

24.

25.

26.

27.

28.

March

Today I Am Thankful For:

1.

2.

3.

4.

5.

6.

7.

8.

Everyday Thanksgiving — Living a Life Full of Gratitude

9.

10.

11.

12.

13.

14.

15.

16.

17.

18.

19.

20.

21.

22.

23.

24.

25.

26.

27.

28.

29.

30.

31.

This month God showed me:

April

Today I Am Thankful For:

1.

2.

3.

4.

5.

6.

7.

8.

Everyday Thanksgiving — Living a Life Full of Gratitude

9.

10.

11.

12.

13.

14.

15.

16.

17.

18.

19.

20.

21.

22.

23.

24.

25.

26.

Everyday Thanksgiving — Living a Life Full of Gratitude

27.

28.

29.

30.

This month God showed me:

May

Today I Am Thankful For:

1.

2.

3.

4.

5.

6.

7.

8.

Everyday Thanksgiving — Living a Life Full of Gratitude

9.

10.

11.

12.

13.

14.

15.

16.

17.

18.

19.

20.

21.

22.

23.

24.

25.

26.

Everyday Thanksgiving — Living a Life Full of Gratitude

27.

28.

29.

30.

31.

This month God showed me:

June

Today I Am Thankful For:

1.

2.

3.

4.

5.

6.

7.

8.

Everyday Thanksgiving — Living a Life Full of Gratitude

9.

10.

11.

12.

13.

14.

15.

16.

17.

18.

19.

20.

21.

22.

23.

24.

25.

26.

Everyday Thanksgiving — Living a Life Full of Gratitude

27.

28.

29.

30.

This month God showed me:

July
Today I Am Thankful For:

1.

2.

3.

4.

5.

6.

7.

8.

Everyday Thanksgiving — Living a Life Full of Gratitude

9.

10.

11.

12.

13.

14.

15.

16.

17.

18.

19.

20.

21.

22.

23.

24.

25.

26.

27.

28.

29.

30.

31.

This month God showed me:

August
Today I Am Thankful For:

1.

2.

3.

4.

5.

6.

7.

8.

9.

10.

11.

12.

13.

14.

15.

16.

17.

18.

19.

20.

21.

22.

23.

24.

25.

26.

Everyday Thanksgiving — Living a Life Full of Gratitude

27.

28.

29.

30.

31.

This month God showed me:

September

Today I Am Thankful For:

1.

2.

3.

4.

5.

6.

7.

8.

Everyday Thanksgiving — Living a Life Full of Gratitude

9.

10.

11.

12.

13.

14.

15.

16.

17.

18.

19.

20.

21.

22.

23.

24.

25.

26.

27.

28.

29.

30.

This month God showed me:

October

Today I Am Thankful For:

1.

2.

3.

4.

5.

6.

7.

8.

Everyday Thanksgiving — Living a Life Full of Gratitude

9.

10.

11.

12.

13.

14.

15.

16.

17.

18.

19.

20.

21.

22.

23.

24.

25.

26.

27.

28.

29.

30.

31.

This month God showed me:

Everyday Thanksgiving — Living a Life Full of Gratitude

That's a Wrap

Soul Friends, it has been such a joy to share this Bible study with you. Please know that you have been prayed over and I am so thankful for you!

To wrap up our study time on Everyday Thanksgiving, I want to leave you with these thoughts from A.W. Tozer:

Gratitude
IS AN OFFERING PRECIOUS IN THE SIGHT OF GOD, AND IT IS ONE THAT THE POOREST OF US CAN MAKE AND BE NOT POORER BUT RICHER FOR HAVING MADE IT.

As we go forward ...

Let's hold on to the truths from God's Word about His faithfulness and continue to pray with the expectation of God delivering an answer to our prayers.

Blessings Soul Friends,

Meet the Authors

Jana Kennedy-Spicer is a wife, mom and Nana who is passionate about inspiring and encouraging women on their daily walk with Christ. A woman rescued and repaired by the grace of God, she loves to share about the realness of God's love, redemption and faithfulness. Embarking on a new life journey, she is dedicated to using her blogging, Bible teaching, writing, photography, drawing, painting and graphic designs to bring glory to the Lord.

Jana teaches Bible Study and Bible Journaling in the Dallas, Texas area. To connect with Jana, visit www.SweetToTheSoul.com or email her directly at jana@sweettothesoul.com.

Jodie Barrett is a wife, mother, homemaker, office manager, teacher and speaker! She resides in the small town of Roanoke Rapids, NC and attends Calvary Baptist Church. She enjoys using the gifts that God has given her combined with the wisdom gained from the Word and life experiences to motivate and encourage women to strengthen their faith and fitness.

Catch up with Jodie on her blog at FaithfullyFollowingMinistries.org.

Additional Resources
FOR EVERYDAY THANKSGIVING

Bible Journaling Kit

Bible Journaling Templates

Scripture Color Pages

Print and Share Scripture Cards

and more .....

For more information visit:
SweetToTheSoul.com/Everyday-Thanksgiving

Other Soul Deep Devotionals & Journals from
Sweet To The Soul Ministries

31-Day Devotionals
Let Your Light Shine : Being a Light in a Dark World

31-Day Scripture Journals
New Life
Love Is
Grace
God's Masterpiece
I Believe
Let Your Light Shine
Everyday Thanksgiving
Anchored Hope

7-Day Scripture Journals
Together We're Better
Rest for the Weary Soul
Every Good Gift

For more information visit:
SweetToTheSoul.com/Soul-Deep-Books

Other Soul Inspired Products from
Sweet To The Soul Ministries

Coloring Books
Garden of Life
Love One Another
Bearing Fruit

Bible Study / Journaling Kits

Anchored Hope	*Joy Filled Life*
Bearing Fruit	*Inspiring Women*
I Am Not Alone	*Gracious Words*

Bible Journaling Templates /
Color Your Own Bookmarks

.

Color Pages & Prints

Bible Journaling / Crafting
Digital Kits
Gods' Masterpiece
Bearing Fruit

.

For more information visit:
SweetToTheSoul.com/Soul-Inspired

Visit our Etsy shop at
www.SweetToTheSoulShoppe.com

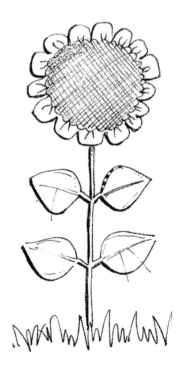

Made in the USA
Columbia, SC
01 November 2024

45490560R00072